A JERRY BRUCKHEIMER PRODUCTION
PIRATES of the CARIBBEAN

ISBN 978-1-4234-8292-5

WALT DISNEY MUSIC COMPANY
WONDERLAND MUSIC COMPANY, INC.

DISTRIBUTED BY

HAL•LEONARD®
CORPORATION
7777 W. BLUEMOUND RD. P.O. BOX 13819 MILWAUKEE, WI 53213

In Australia contact:
Hal Leonard Australia Pty. Ltd.
4 Lentara Court
Cheltenham, Victoria, 3192 Australia
Email: ausadmin@halleonard.com.au

Visit Hal Leonard Online at
www.halleonard.com

Arranged by
Tom Huizinga

Blood Ritual

from Walt Disney Pictures' PIRATES OF THE CARIBBEAN:
THE CURSE OF THE BLACK PEARL

Music by Klaus Badelt

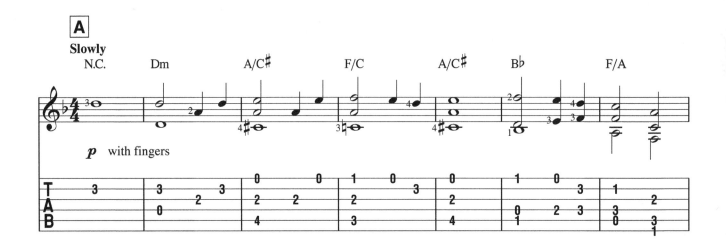

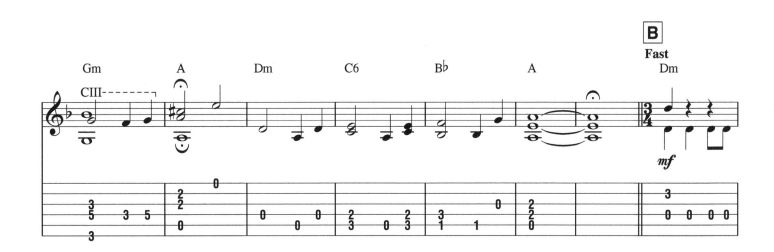

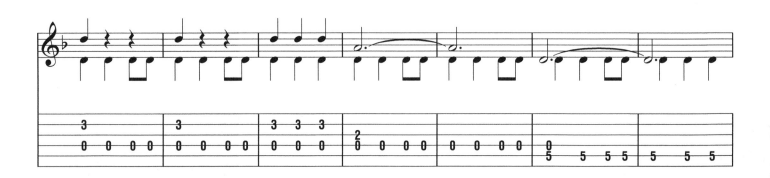

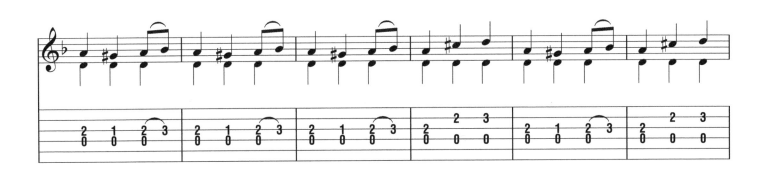

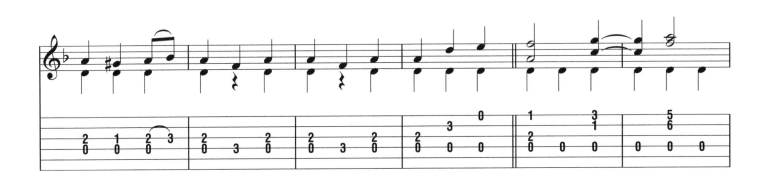

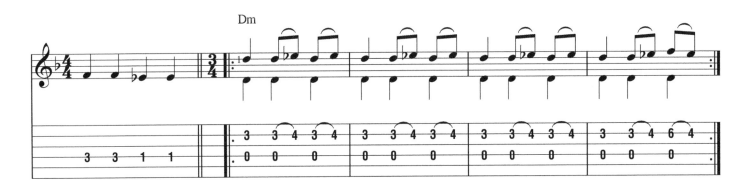

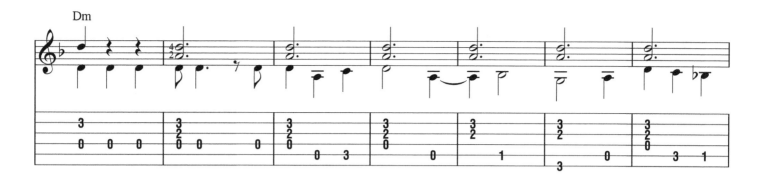

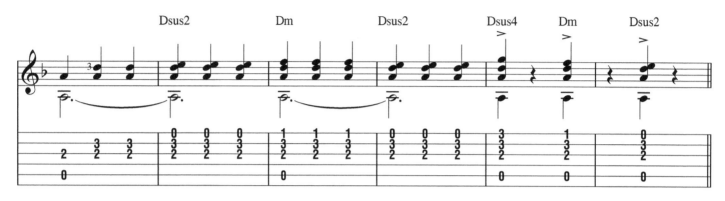

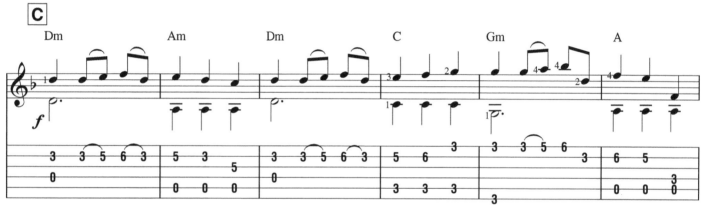

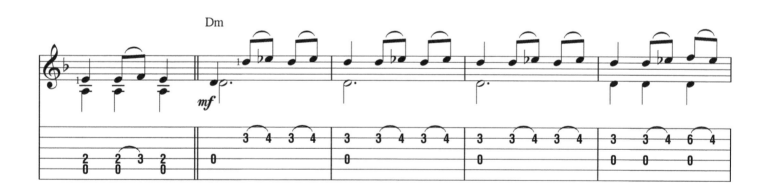

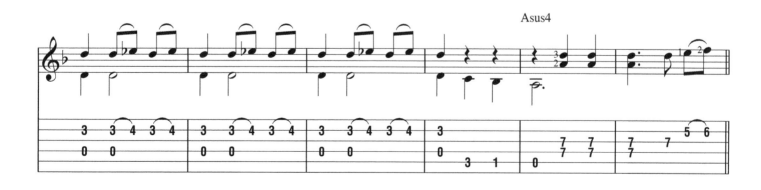

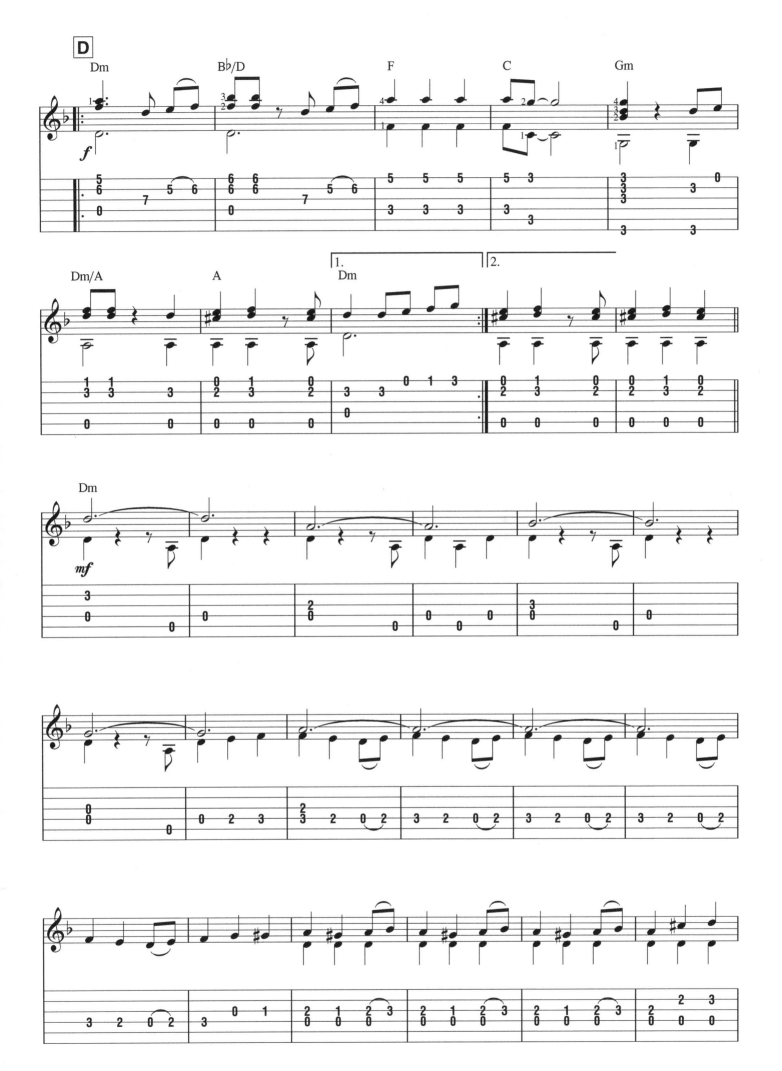

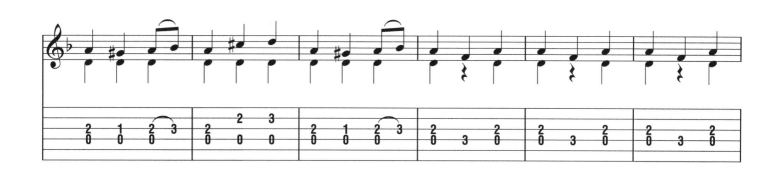

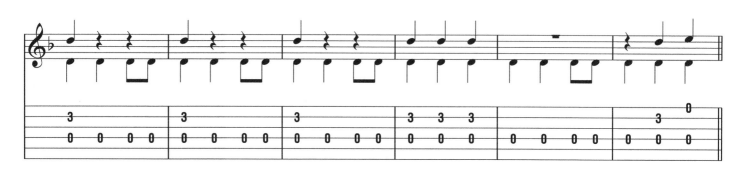

E

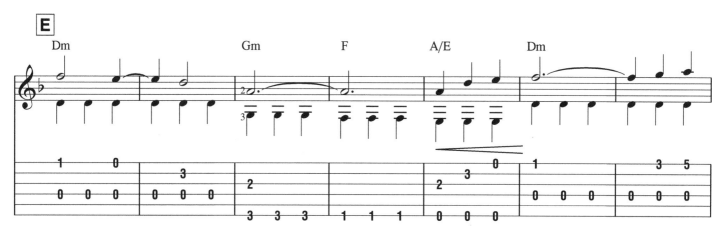

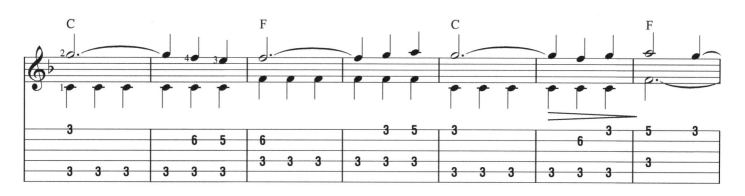

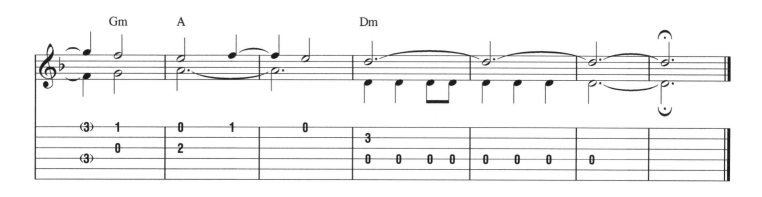

Davy Jones

from Walt Disney Pictures'
PIRATES OF THE CARIBBEAN: DEAD MAN'S CHEST
Music by Hans Zimmer

*Capo V

*Optional: To match recording, place capo at 5th fret.

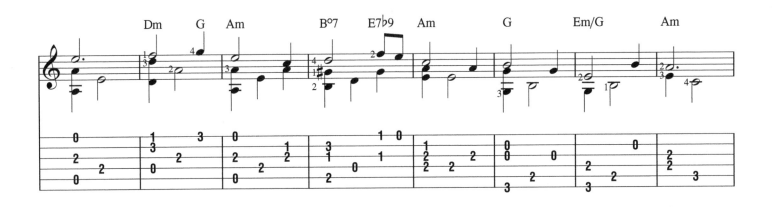

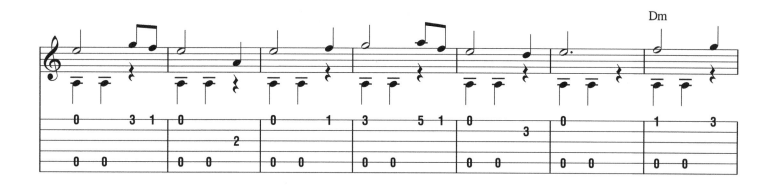

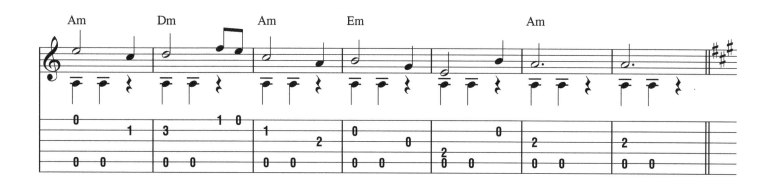

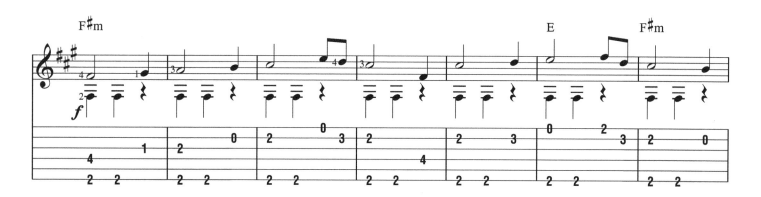

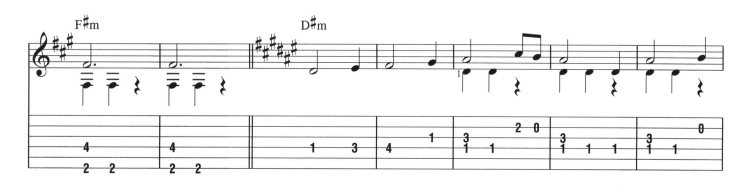

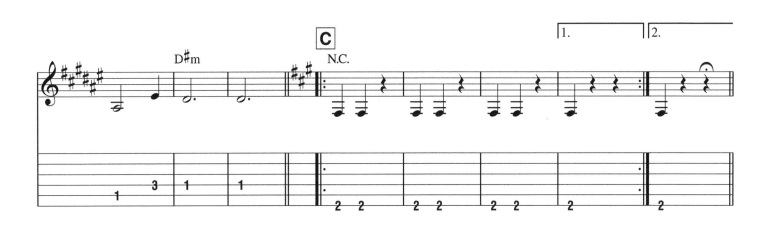

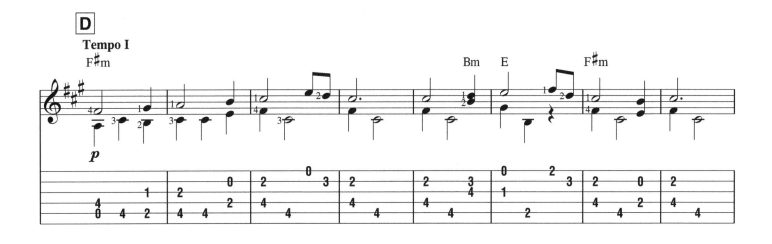

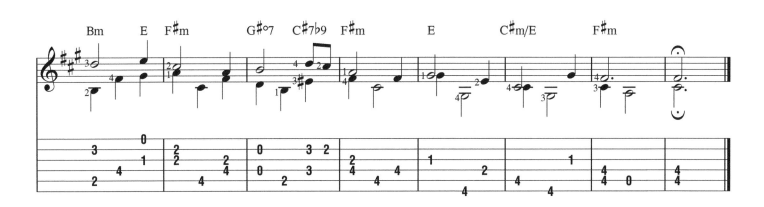

He's a Pirate

from Walt Disney Pictures' PIRATES OF THE CARIBBEAN:
THE CURSE OF THE BLACK PEARL

Music by Klaus Badelt

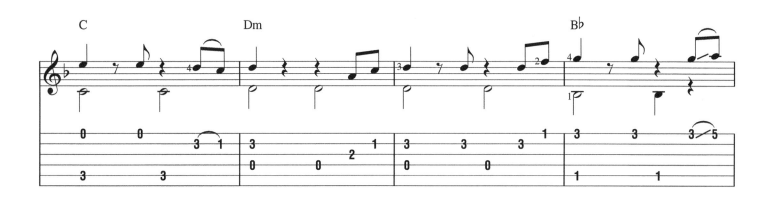

Hoist the Colours

from Walt Disney Pictures'
PIRATES OF THE CARIBBEAN: AT WORLD'S END

Lyrics by Ted Elliot and Terry Rossio
Music by Hans Zimmer and Gore Verbinski

I've Got My Eye on You

from Walt Disney Pictures' PIRATES OF THE CARIBBEAN:
DEAD MAN'S CHEST

Music by Hans Zimmer

Drop D tuning:
(low to high) D-A-D-G-B-E

A

Moderately
N.C.

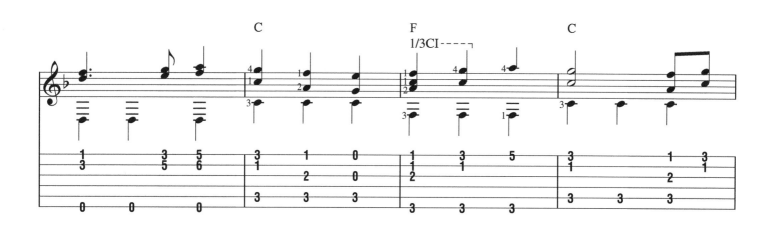

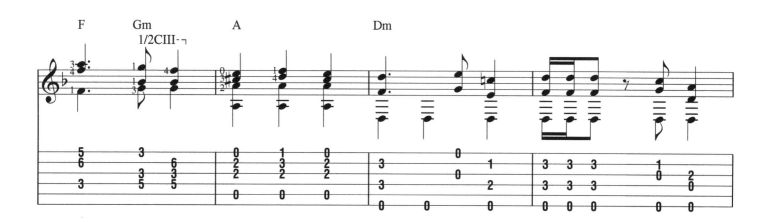

The Medallion Calls

from Walt Disney Pictures' PIRATES OF THE CARIBBEAN:
THE CURSE OF THE BLACK PEARL

Music by Klaus Badelt

Drop D tuning:
(low to high) D-A-D-G-B-E

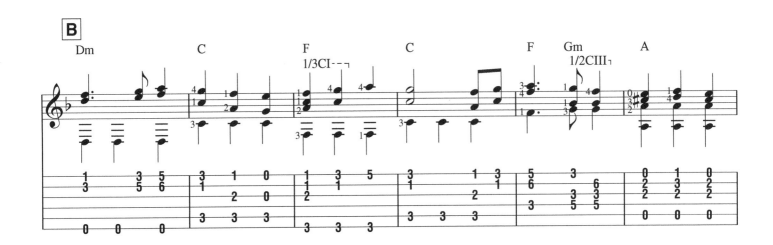

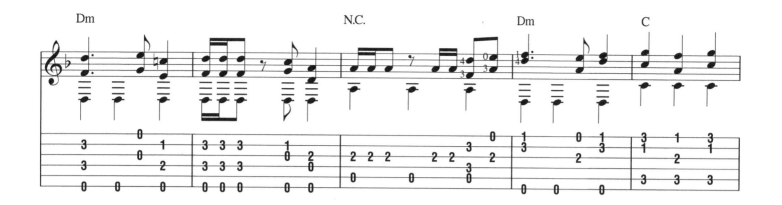

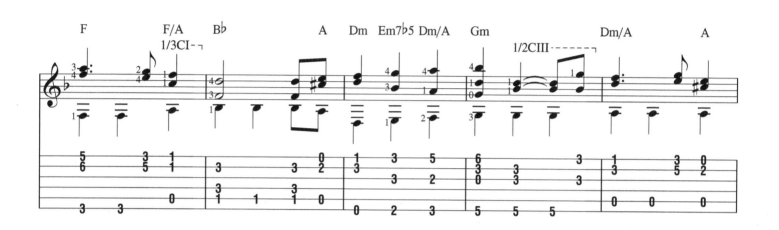

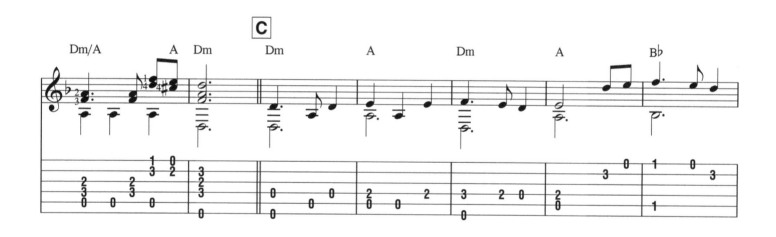

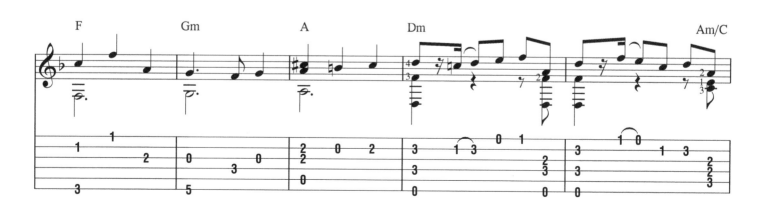

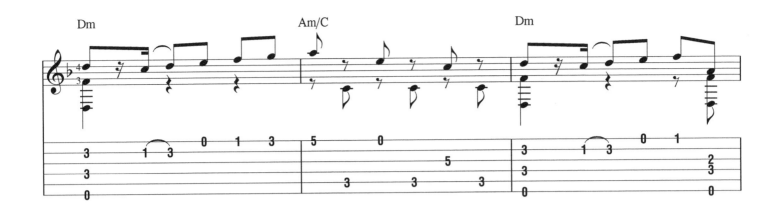

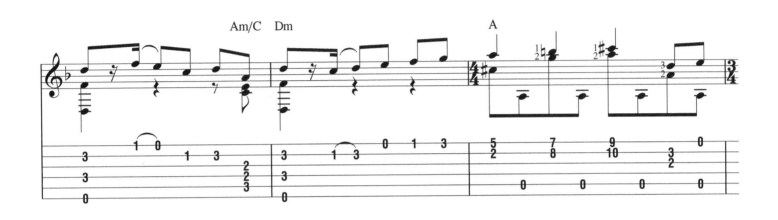

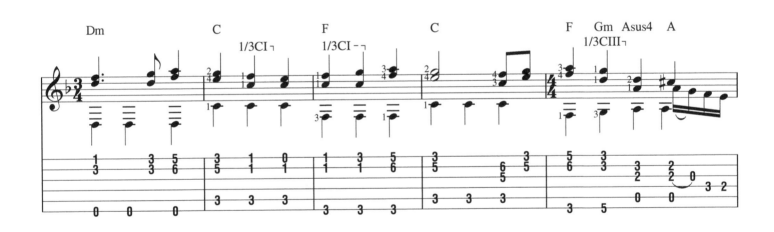

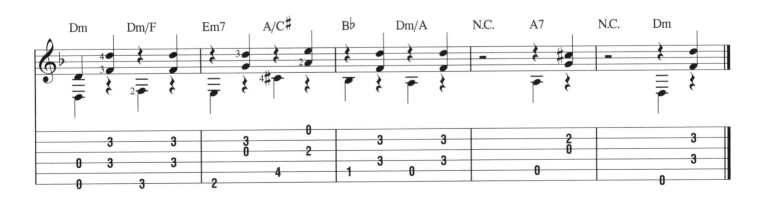

One Day

from Walt Disney Pictures'
PIRATES OF THE CARIBBEAN: AT WORLD'S END

Music by Hans Zimmer

Drop D tuning:
(low to high) D-A-D-G-B-E

A

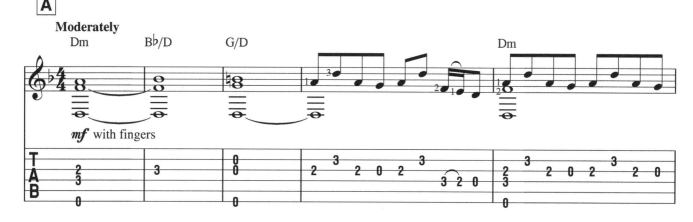

Moonlight Serenade

from Walt Disney Pictures' PIRATES OF THE CARIBBEAN:
THE CURSE OF THE BLACK PEARL

Music by Klaus Badelt

Drop D tuning:
(low to high) D-A-D-G-B-E

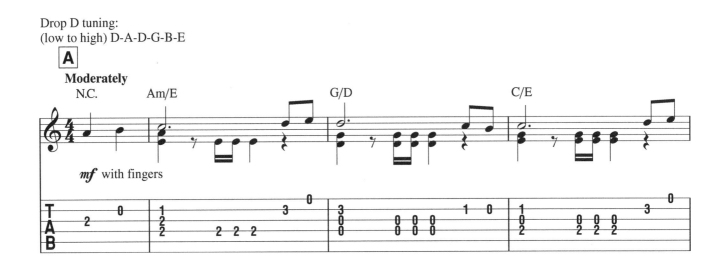

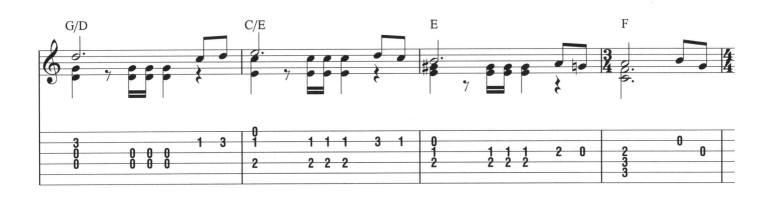

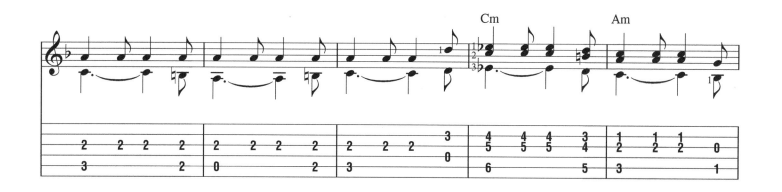

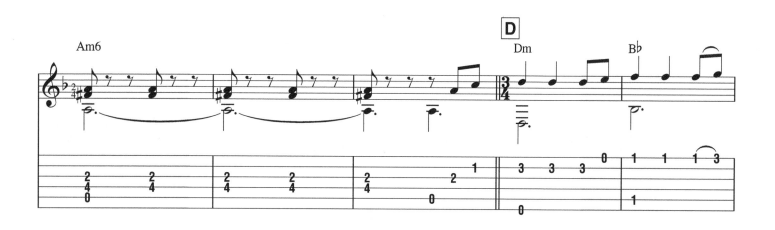

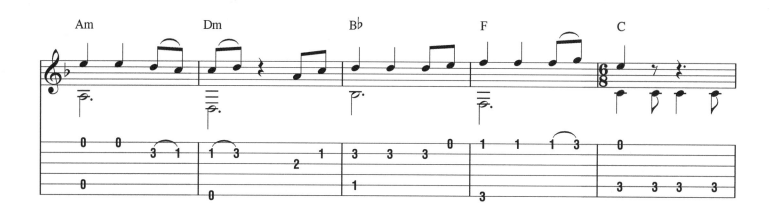

Two Hornpipes

(Fisher's Hornpipe)

from Walt Disney Pictures'
PIRATES OF THE CARIBBEAN: DEAD MAN'S CHEST
By Skip Henderson

*Optional: To match recording, place capo at 2nd fret.

Up Is Down

from Walt Disney Pictures'
PIRATES OF THE CARIBBEAN: AT WORLD'S END
Music by Hans Zimmer

Drop D tuning:
(low to high) D-A-D-G-B-E

*Chords in parentheses reflect implied harmony.